knot it!

To my mother, for her enduring support; she, among other things, inspired me to be creative. And to my father, who, among other things, inspired me to learn my knots and run my own business.

FAMILIUS

Published by Familius LLC, www.familius.com

Familius books are available at special discounts for bulk purchases, whether for sales promotions or for family or corporate use. For more information, contact Familius Sales at 559-876-2170 or email orders@familius.com.

Library of Congress Cataloging-in-Publication Data
2018937157   Hardcover ISBN 9781945547737   Ebook ISBN 9781641700894

Edited by Lacey Kupfer Wulf
Cover design by David Miles
Book design by Kurt Wahlner and David Miles
Illustrations by John Sherry

Printed in China

10 9 8 7 6 5 4

First Edition

CAUTION: Any activity involving rope can be dangerous and may even be life threatening! Knot illustrations contained in this book are not intended for rock-climbing instruction. Many knots are not suitable for the risks involved in climbing, rescue work, or dangerous activities. Where failure could cause property damage, injury, or death, seek professional instruction prior to use. Many factors affect knots, including the appropriateness of knots and rope materials used in particular applications; the age, size, and condition of ropes; and the accuracy with which these descriptions have been followed. Inspect all knots before and during use. Further, all knots reduce the overall strength of a rope to varying degrees. No responsibility is accepted for incidents arising from the use of this content.

CONTENTS

INTRODUCTION

MOST ROPE KNOTS TRACE THEIR ORIGIN back to the age of sail, but the ability to tie knots still holds relevance in this day and age and is an invaluable skill to possess. Just find yourself with a rope in hand and a task for that rope, and you will be glad you learned a few of the knots in this book. With the confidence this knowledge often inspires, you may even find yourself becoming a modern-day knot aficionado!

Accompanying this book of one hundred useful knots is a set of Pro-Knot Best Rope Knot cards. The original concept of the knot cards was to provide easy-to-understand illustrations of some essential knots on cards that were a handy size, portable, and waterproof. That concept has proven successful, with over one million knot cards sold. This book expands upon those twenty knots but maintains the emphasis of providing clear, concise tying instructions. You won't find long-winded dissertations of a knot's history here. You also won't find a lot of anecdotal stories or a history lesson about rope. What you will find is a logical layout of one hundred carefully chosen knots with a short description and use of each knot, along with an easy-to-follow, step-by-step illustration of how to tie the knot. These knots will serve you well for all indoor and outdoor activities, from camping and fishing to climbing, sailing, search-and-rescue, and beyond.

The twenty best knots that are on the included knot cards are highlighted in the text of the book. A few of the best fishing knots have been included as well. Bear in mind that it is more important to learn a few knots well than to half-learn all of the knots. Keep the knot cards handy for when the memory gets a little rusty and you are out in the field needing to tie the right knot. Enjoy!

ROPE KNOTS

Rope knots are grouped according to their function. "Hitches" are used to tie a rope to an object, such as a post or a cleat. "Bends" are knots that are used to join two ropes together. "Loops" are knots that make, as their name implies, a loop in a rope. "Binding Knots" are used to secure loose objects together. A few knots are listed in a "Special Purpose Knots" category, such as stopper knots, whip finishes, and coils.